JUBBA JAWS PUBLISHING

Lynda Randle Ministries
c/o Jubba Jaws Publishing
5559 NW Barry Road, PMB 236
Kansas City, MO 64154

ISBN: 978-0-692-62072-4

Printed in the United States of America

This edition first printing, February 2016

Designed by Kimberly R. Hines

The Cab Driver's Daughter

Written by

Lynda Randle

Illustrated by

Diana Rendell

JUBBA JAWS PUBLISHING

2016

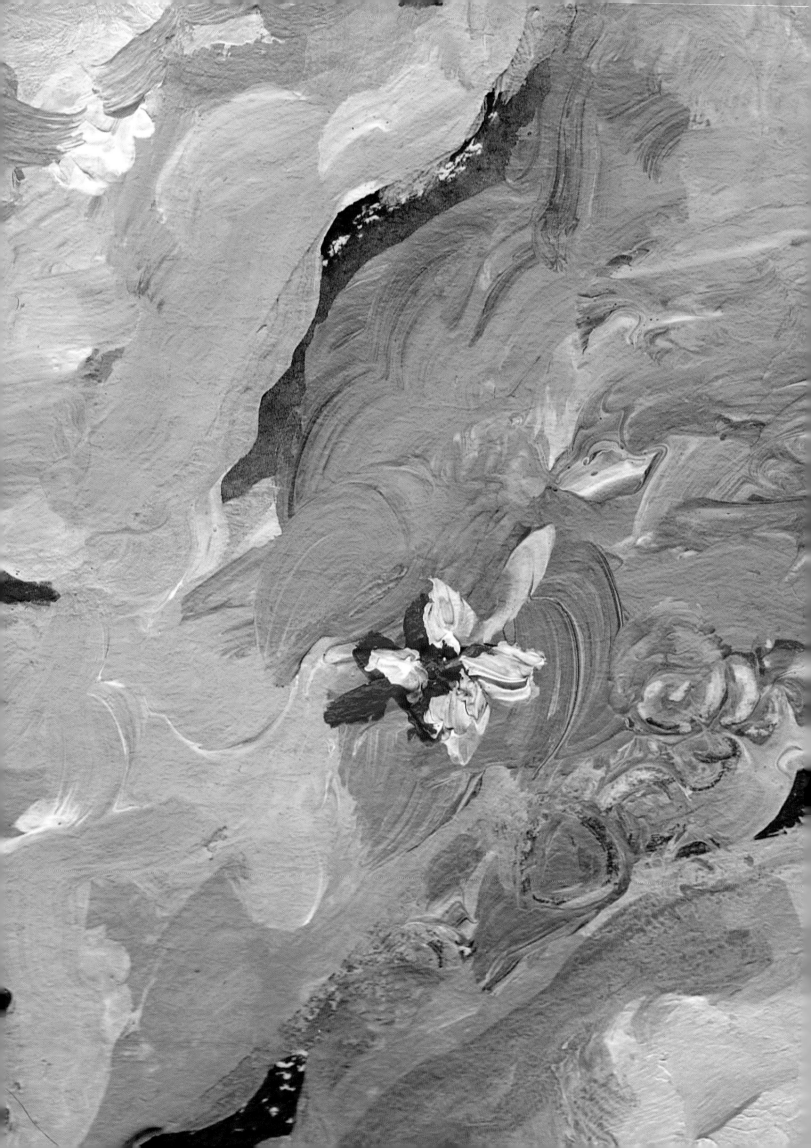

Thank you **GOD** for the gift of your Son, **JESUS CHRIST**!
He changed this cab driver's daughter's life FOREVER! Oh how I love you Jesus!!

To my handsome husband **Michael Randle**
and our two beautiful daughters, **Patience Erin** and **Joy Danielle**!
Your love and support means everything to me!
Thank you for inspiring me to live ABOVE and BEYOND and to DREAM BIG!
I love you all so very deep. Patience and Joy, your dad and I can't wait to read this book
to your kids, (our grandchildren) when that time comes!

To all of my siblings, **Bill**, **Sharyn**, **Ann**, **Angie**, **Nathel** and **Michael**,
I am glad that we grew up in the same household together!
It made me the woman I am today and the woman
that I am becoming with each day that passes! I love you all!

Diana Rendell, Who knew? Your Illustrations are AMAZING!
Thank you for all of the many hours you spent bringing my story to life
on the pages of this book! Now the whole world will see why I love my Jesus so!
What an incredible talent you are and I am so glad that you said 'yes'!
Love and Hugs, my newfound sister and friend!

Mom and Dad, this book would not have ever been written
had you not come to the saving knowledge of Jesus!
Thank you for staying together and allowing Jesus
to mend your broken hearts, broken home and marriage!
And I'm SO glad that you decided to have 6 more kids!
I love and miss you both beyond words!!

Mom and Dad Randle, thank you for giving birth to my hubby
and for teaching him the fear of the Lord at a very early age!
And thank you for being the best mom and dad–in love–that any woman could ever have!
We miss you too so very much and we love you with all our hearts!

THIS BOOK IS DEDICATED TO:

My handsome 'Princes' and great nephews,
Dayveonn Ja'Vell Tait and **Kaydenn Maxwell Tait**
and to my gorgeous little 'Princesses' and great nieces,
Madison Christine Tait and **A'Niah Renee' Randle**!
Auntie Lynda loves you all so very much and I pray
that you will grow up to love Jesus with all of your hearts
and NEVER ever forget just how much He loves you!
Remember that you can DREAM BIG too!

My godchild **Sydney Grace Williams**, god mommy really loves you
and I feel so blessed and privileged to be a part of your life and world!
You are growing up to be an amazing young lady and I am super proud of you!
Keep your eyes on Jesus, baby girl! DREAM BIG!

Once upon a time on Capitol Hill
lived a husband and wife and their little boy, Bill.

The husband's name was Nate and he drove a cab.
It was bright, sparkly yellow. Oh, it was so fab!

The wife's name was Maxine
and she was a dream.
She stayed home with Bill.
She cooked and she cleaned.

They were happy for a while,
but things quickly changed.
You see, neither of them knew Jesus.
They had never believed on His name.

So Nate left Maxine
with their little boy Bill.
They moved to North Carolina.
But, Nate stayed on the Hill.

Oh, but he was so sad,
and the tears began to flow.
He wished they had stayed.

Why did he let them go?

So, he got in his cab.
He wanted to think and drive
away from the Hill
right on the Maryland Line.

He turned on the radio
and to his surprise,
he was hearing The Gospel
for the very first time.

He heard a man preaching.
His name was Oliver B Green.
He said...

So Nate pulled over his cab
and accepted Christ into his heart.
He finally met Jesus
now his new life would start.

When he made it home, later that day,
he picked up the phone to call Maxine and say,
"Honey, I was wrong. Can you and Bill please come home?
I heard about Jesus today on the Gospel radio."

"He can put us back together
and fix all the broken parts,
if you will believe on His name
and accept Him into your heart."

So Maxine and little Bill
asked Jesus into their hearts,
then they moved back on the Hill.
Now their new life would start.

It didn't take long
for their family to grow.
They had a lot more kids.
And what do you know?

SIX to be exact.
And I was smack dab in the middle.
The cab driver's daughter.
Oh, I was so little!

Life got even better because, as a family, we would pray, gathered around our kitchen table each and every new day.

I got to learn about Jesus at a very early age,
and it didn't take long before I, too, was saved.

I remember so well.
It seems just like yesterday.
I was sitting around the kitchen table,
when I heard my dad say,

"Pray this prayer with me, 'Chub',
(as I was fondly known)

"*Jesus, come live in my heart.
Please make it your home.*"

So that's exactly what I did
and I was only 12 at the time,
but it's still the best decision
I ever made in my life.

There were so many things I enjoyed as a kid, like going to school and playing with my friends.

I loved going to church
and worshipping the Lord,
sometimes in praise dance
and sometimes with my voice.

I loved playing with my brothers
and my sisters, too.
Never a dull moment,
there was so much to do.

And watching my mom cook
was always a delight—
seemed like everything she made
came out just right.

But the time I enjoyed most
was being with my dad,
picking up all kinds of passengers
in his bright, sparkly yellow taxicab.

He was always so kind
to each one who entered.

His words were so loving,

always Christ-centered.

I don't think he realized
how much I was learning,
listening to him talk
as the wheels were turning.

His love for Jesus
was so deep and so strong.
He would share The Gospel message
nearly all the day long.

But somewhere along the way,
I got off track.
I started getting into trouble
and going down the wrong path.

But my mom and my dad
believed in the power of prayer,
So they turned to Jesus and let go of their cares.

Then they made a decision
to put me in a Christian school.
I wasn't too happy.
I didn't think it was cool.

They didn't have the classes
that I wanted to take,
so I ended up in the choir,
and I had the only chocolate face.

There were so many kids
who didn't look like me.
Their skin was much lighter
like vanilla ice cream.

But it didn't take long
for me to make new friends,
'cause I was taught to love people
no matter the color of their skin.

I remembered the words
of my mom and dad.

"God loves us all
and that's a fact."

So, I did my best
and got back on track.
I studied hard
and stayed on the right path.

Then I started singing
all over town,
and people would come
from all around.

"If you don't mean it, don't sing it."

is what my dad used to say.
And I've never forgotten that
even to this day.

I knew my voice
was a gift from God,
and He wanted me to use it
to spread His love.

So, that's just what I did
every chance that I got.
I sang of God's goodness
because I loved Him a lot.

And when I got to go to college,
I continued to sing,
because I knew my mom and dad
wanted me to pursue my dreams.

Many years have passed
since my college days, and
I'm so grateful to God
for the prayers my parents prayed.

And now I'm all grown up
and I've got a family of my own,
a husband and two beautiful daughters,
and we have a Christian home.

And I'm still singing all over the world
and across many beautiful waters.

And, who would ever, ever believe

that I was just a cab driver's daughter?

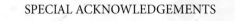

SPECIAL ACKNOWLEDGEMENTS

Jay Rouse, thank you for doing a brilliant job on the sound track for my narration!
It was such a delight and pleasure working with you
and I look forward to our next musical collaboration!

Kimberly Hines, you are truly a godsend!
This book would still be waiting to be laid out, 'photoshopped', spell-checked
and all of the in-betweens, had you not stepped in when you did!
Thank you for coming to our aid and for bringing your many gifts to the table!
I love you my dear sister and friend!

**Donna Butler, JoAnne Heinke, Jeanne Tucker, Regina Crutcher,
Tim Kaufmann, Bill and Gloria Gaither, LD and Marilyn Davis,
Gina Brisco, Sue Plummer** and **Linda Robuck.**
Thank you is the understatement!
You've all sown into my life and ministry in one way or another
and I could never repay you for all the many ways you've invested in me!
I love you all so very much and I praise God for putting you in my life!
May your rewards be great on this earth and in heaven!

Jimmy Moody, may our Lord bless and keep you
and make His face shine upon you and give you peace!
Thank you for everything!
Remember how much you are loved and prayed for my friend!
Lots of love!

Dad Leach and **Ron Lord**, I miss you so very much!
Our long awaited book has finally come to fruition.
You both told me how great it would be
and I wish you could be here to see it launch!
I know that you are watching from the portals of heaven
as it gets into the hands of people all around the world!
Heaven is certainly sweeter because you are there!
I will ALWAYS love you!

And lastly I would like to thank all of the administrators, teachers and professors
at **Riverdale Baptist Christian School** and **Liberty University**!
Attending your school and university was life altering!
Only God knows where I would be had my parents not made that 'dreadful' decision
to put me in a Christian School and University!
Thank you for investing in my life and eternal destiny!